The Rain Forest

People of the
Rain Forest

Mae Woods
ABDO Publishing Company

visit us at
www.abdopub.com

Published by Abdo Publishing Company 4940 Viking Drive, Edina, Minnesota 55435.
Copyright © 1999 by Abdo Consulting Group, Inc. International copyrights reserved in all
countries. No part of this book may be reproduced in any form without written permission
from the publisher.

Printed in the United States.

Photo credits: Peter Arnold, Inc.

Edited by Lori Kinstad Pupeza
Contributing editor Morgan Hughes
Graphics by Linda O'Leary

Library of Congress Cataloging-in-Publication Data

Woods, Mae.
     People of the rain forest / Mae Woods.
     p. cm. -- (The rain forest)
     Includes index.
     Summary: Describes how different groups of peoples live in rain
     forests in Central and South America, Africa, and Southeast Asia.
     ISBN 1-57765-020-4
     1. Rain forest people--Juvenile literature. 2. Rain forest ecology--
Juvenile literature. [1. Rain forest people. 2. Human geography.] I.
Title. II. Series: Woods, Mae. Rain forest.
     GN394.W66 1999
     577.34--dc21
                                                               98-9982
                                                               CIP
                                                               AC

Note to reader
The words in the text that are the color green refer to the words in the glossary.

Contents

Living in the Rain Forest

There are about 1,000 different groups of native peoples living in the rain forests of Central and South America, Africa, and Southeast Asia. Some have been around for 40,000 years. These people live differently, but they share many customs. They wear very little clothing because it is hot. Many decorate their bodies. They wear jewelry made of seeds, feathers, animal teeth, or bone. Some native peoples paint on their skin.

Native people live in harmony with the environment. They gather fruits, nuts, and vegetables. They also farm crops, hunt, and fish. Native peoples know which plants contain poison and which animals are dangerous.

They use trees to build homes and to make tools and weapons. They know how to make medicine from plants. Today, scientists are studying native peoples to learn more about the rain forests.

Children begin learning at a young age about their native customs.

5

Customs and Family Life

*M*ost native peoples live in small family groups. Each group has a chief and may have a medicine man. A medicine man helps sick or hurt people get better. Groups who hunt and gather food live in camps miles away from each other. Each group needs its own area so there will be enough food for everyone.

Native groups who farm live in villages. People help each other to build their houses and to raise their children. Every man, woman, and child has work to do.

All people living in rain forests have rituals. Some celebrate hunting and sharing food. Most groups have special celebrations for birth, growing up, marriage, and death. They wear bright costumes, headdresses, or masks during these celebrations. They may dance and sing as part of the rituals.

As they grow up, children are taught the customs of their people. They also learn about rain forest animals, plants, and soil. Later, they will pass on this knowledge to their own children.

The Indonesian Asmats have rituals
that celebrate hunting and fishing.

American Indians

Many groups of American Indians live in Central and South America. In early times, these American Indians were fierce warriors. Now, American Indians are hunters, farmers, or traders.

The largest American Indian group is the Yanomamo. Some people live in the hills in round houses made of sticks, vines, and leaves. Other groups live by rivers in houses built on stilts. If the water rises, it will not flood their homes. The American Indians make canoes from trees. They travel deep into forests and hunt near riversides. Hunters use bows and arrows. They make cutting tools from the sharp teeth of large rats.

Traders make carved dolls, necklaces, and other jewelry. They spin cloth and weave baskets using the fibers of plants and vines. These goods can be traded for food, clothing, or tools with other people. This form of buying and selling without using money is called bartering.

8

Central and South America

**Mud-covered children in the Amazon basin
tropical rain forest in South America.**

Africans

*T*he first people in the African rain forest were the Pygmies. Pygmies still live in Zaire. They are **nomads**. Every few weeks they move to new areas to hunt. Pygmies are also very small in size. One group, the Mbuti (Embooty), are less than 5 feet (1.5 meters) tall as adults. Mbuti call the rain forest "mother" or "father" in their language. Hunters offer a prayer of thanks to the forest before eating meat.

Mbuti are **skilled** artists. The men peel the bark from trees, soak it in water, then pound it into a soft cloth. The women paint designs on bark using **dyes** made from plants. These bark cloths are worn during ceremonies. Babies are wrapped in bark cloth to give them the blessings from the forest. Mbuti love to sing. They create music with rattles and drums. They have songs for special events, such as gathering honey or hunting animals.

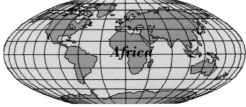

Ituri rain forest, pygmy chief playing a drum.

Pacific Island People

Many native people live on islands in the Pacific Ocean. There are people living in rain forests in Malaysia, Indonesia, and New Guinea as well as in Southeast Asia and Australia. Some live very simply. They use tools made of stone and have no weapons. They eat fish, frogs, insects, and nuts.

Also in this area are those who live more modern lives. The Iban live in villages in large cleared areas. They go into the rain forests to hunt. They also collect vines to make baskets. Iban men are good craftsmen. They make beautiful silver jewelry. The women weave clothes and rugs. The whole group lives together in a long house. This building is as long as a city block and built on stilts.

In the past, Iban warriors were headhunters. Today, they are known for their art, dance, and costumes. They welcome people who come from cities to buy their crafts.

Many native people make baskets and crafts out of vines that they collect from rain forests.

Building Homes

*I*n African rain forests, Pygmies live in small, dome shaped huts. These huts are built by the women and children of the families. They join sticks to form an A-shaped frame. Then they cover it with palm **fronds**, leaves, and branches. Pygmies stay in one camp as long as there is plenty of food. When they move to another hunting ground, they build new homes.

In the thick jungles of South America and Asia, native people clear the trees from large areas to form villages. They build their houses high above the ground. This protects them from floods and the fierce animals who roam about at night in search of food. The houses are made of **timber**, bamboo, and palm leaves. Their **thatched roofs** slope to drain off the rain. The roofs are made by **skillfully** weaving branches and leaves into thick coverings.

This house in the Amazon rain forest is made of wood
and roofed with palm tree leaves.

Hunting

Rain forest natives hunt for food. They make weapons from plants and trees. The stems of long palm leaves are bent into bows. Branches are sharpened to make arrows and spears. Sometimes hunters wet the tips in poison taken from plants or skins of poisonous frogs. Hunters also use blowpipes made from hollow reeds. They blow darts through the pipes to kill birds and other small animals.

Hunters travel in small groups using their pet dogs to help them track the wild animals. They hunt deer, **capybara**, pigs, antelope, and wild birds. When boys are about five years old, they begin to join their fathers in the hunts.

Hunters have a clever way of catching fish. They build underwater fences out of branches and vines. This special net traps the largest fish as they swim downstream. After a day of hunting in the forest, hunters return to the rivers and add the day's catch to the dinner they are bringing home.

An Asmat hunter in an Indonesian rain forest.

Farming

Native peoples who farm know that rain forest soil lacks **nutrients**. They mix nests of termites and ants into the dirt as a **fertilizer**. Sometimes they burn down the trees then plant **crops** in the ash that is left. The ash is food for the soil.

Farmers also know natural ways to protect crops from pests. They control leaf-cutter ants by planting banana trees nearby. The trees attract wasps. Wasps will attack the ants before they can eat the crops.

Farmers cannot plant in the same soil for more than three years. When the nutrients are used up, the plants die. Then farmers move to new areas. The old garden is left to grow wild. A few years later it will be part of the rain forest again.

In Asia, the farmers grow rice in **paddies** along rivers. Rice farmers do not need to move because the fresh water brings nutrients to each new crop.

A father and his children preparing wheat.

Food

*I*n the rain forests, fruits and vegetables grow all year long. Native peoples never need to store food. Hunters and farmers share their meat and crops with each other.

In Southeast Asia, rice is the main food eaten. In the Amazon and in Africa, a lot of people eat manioc, also called cassava. Manioc is a white vegetable, similar to a potato. The manioc plant is poisonous. Native people have discovered a way to prepare the root so they can eat it. They soak it in water, then grate it. They press it into round patties. These are cooked until crisp and eaten like bread.

People who live in rain forests often eat fish, meat, and the eggs of wild birds. They cook with palm oil and hot spices. They also eat beans, corn, and yams. Plantain, a type of banana, is cooked and eaten with meals. They also eat fruits, berries, nuts, seeds, and honey.

This family in the Amazon rain forest is peeling potato-like vegetables called manioc.

Glossary

Capybara - a large animal in the rat family that lives near water.

Celebrate - to honor a special event with a party or ceremony.

Crops - plants grown for food.

Custom - something a person usually does; habit or tradition.

Dye - a paint material used to add new colors to cloth, hair, or skin.

Environment - all the things that surround a person, animal, or plant and affect its health.

Fertilizer - food for plants that is added to soil.

Fiber - a threadlike part of a plant.

Frond - the leaf of a fern or palm.

Grate - to shred into bits by rubbing against a rough surface.

Harmony - peace; a friendly relationship.

Headhunters - warriors who keep the heads of people they kill.

Manioc - a white, starchy vegetable similar to a potato.

Nomads - people who move and have no permanent home.

Nutrients - matter needed for the growth of plants or animals.

Paddy - a field covered in water where rice is grown.

Ritual - a set form of rites; a ceremony.

Skilled - trained; done well because a worker has had much practice.

Thatched roof - the covering of a home made of interwoven straw, sticks, or palm leaves.

Timber - wood used for building.

Internet Sites

Amazon Interactive
http://www.eduweb.com/amazon.html
Explore the geography of the Ecuadorian rain forest through on-line games and activities. Discover the ways in which the Quichua live off the land.

Living Edens: Manu, Peru's Hidden Rain Forest
http://www.pbs.org/edens/manu/
This site is about the animals and indigenous people who populate Peru's Manu region.

The Rain Forest Workshop
http://kids.osd.wednet.edu/Marshall/rainforest_home_page.html
The Rain Forest Workshop was developed by Virginia Reid and the students at Thurgood Marshall Middle School in Olympia, Washington. This site is one of the best school sites around with links to many other sites as well as great information on the rain forest.

The Tropical Rain Forest in Suriname
http://www.euronet.nl/users/mbleeker/suriname/suri-eng.html
A multimedia tour through the rain forest in Suriname (SA). Read about plants, animals, Indians, and Maroons. This site is very organized and full of information.

These sites are subject to change. Go to your favorite search engine and type in Rain Forest for more sites.

Pass It On

Rain Forest Enthusiasts: educate readers around the country by passing on information you've learned about rain forests. Share your little-known facts and interesting stories. Tell others about animals, insects, or people of the rain forest. We want to hear from you!

To get posted on the ABDO Publishing Company's website E-mail us at "Science@abdopub.com"
Visit the ABDO Publishing Company website at www.abdopub.com

Index